Series Editor: Rosalind Kerven

Heinemann Educational Publishers
Halley Court, Jordan Hill, Oxford OX2 8EJ

MADRID   ATHENS   PARIS
FLORENCE   PRAGUE   WARSAW
PORTSMOUTH NH   CHICAGO   SAO PAULO
SINGAPORE   TOKYO   MELBOURNE   AUCKLAND
IBADAN   GABORONE   JOHANNESBURG

© Heinemann Educational 1995

First published 1995

99 98 97 96 95
10 9 8 7 6 5 4 3 2 1

British Library Cataloguing in Publication Data
A catalogue record for this book is available from the British Library

Starter Pack
1 of each of 12 titles: ISBN 0 435 00957 5

Library Hardback
Fire!: ISBN 0 431 06509 8
Pack 1 – 1 each of 6 titles: ISBN 0 431 06498 9
Pack 2 – 1 each of 6 titles: ISBN 0 431 06499 7

Typeset by Sue Vaudin
Printed and bound in Hong Kong

Acknowledgements
Title page and border illustration, pp 2/3: Hilary Evans;
map and illustration, pp 2/3: Dave Bowyer; photograph, p3: Robert Harding

Fire!

Retold by Rosalind Kerven
Illustrated by Annabel Large
Series Editor: Rosalind Kerven

Introduction

The Aborigine people have lived in Australia for many thousands of years.

In the old days they lived by gathering wild food and hunting.

Their tools and houses were very simple, but their ideas about the world and religion were complex.

About 200 years ago many people from Europe moved to Australia.

They took all the best land and made the Aborigines live like them.

Map of Australia

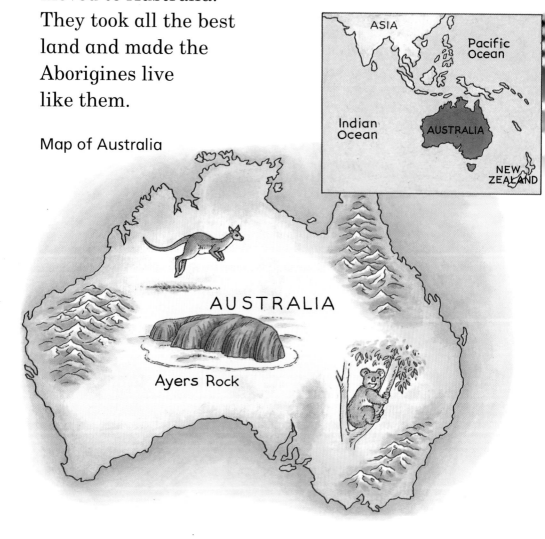

Stories from the Dream Time

Although the lives of young Aboriginal children are very different today, stories are an important part of Aborigine religion.

Many of them talk about the 'Dream Time' - a lost time in the past when great spirits were creating and shaping the world.

The characters are often half-human, half-animal.

Many of them are 'totems' - sacred spirit-animals who protected the people.

Making a fire without matches

Think of Fire.

Think of warmth on a cold night.

Think of bright flames, chasing away the shadows.

Think of hot roasted food,

dripping with delicious juices.

Yes, Fire is happiness and comfort!

Ah, so now imagine a world without Fire.

There was no Fire long ago in the Dream-Time.
In those days,
great spirits walked across the empty land,
making rivers, rocks, plants and living creatures.
In the beginning,
this whole new world was cold and dark.

Suddenly -
a flame appeared.
It lit up the night
like a dazzling flash of sunlight.
But, before it could grow and burn more brightly,
seven greedy hands reached out
and snatched it away!

6

These hands belonged to seven spirit-women
called the Karak-Karak sisters.
As soon as they saw the first flash of Fire,
they wanted to keep this precious, beautiful thing
all for themselves.

7

A spirit-man called Wakala
heard about the Karak-Karak women's secret.
He made up his mind to steal it from them.

One day, these women were walking past his camp,
"Hello there!" called Wakala in a friendly way.
"Come and sit with me! Come and share my meal!"

The Karak-Karak women liked Wakala.
The next day, they went out to gather
some food for themselves,
and let Wakala walk beside them.
They didn't realize he was
only pretending to be friendly
because he wanted to discover their secret.

Wakala watched the spirit-women
use their digging sticks to find roots
and insects in the ground.
He saw that each time they swung the sticks down
the ends flashed with hidden sparks of Fire.
So that was where they kept it!

That night, Wakala and the women sat talking again.
"Tell me," said Wakala, "What is your favourite food?"
"Nothing tastes nicer than fat juicy termites," said one.
"Mind you, we like most things," said another woman.
"But not snakes," said a third.
All the women shrieked.
"Ugh, no! Snakes are terrible, squirmy, scary things!"

11

Wakala fell asleep laughing quietly to himself.
The next morning he went off alone
and caught a big bundle of snakes.
He didn't kill them,
but hid them inside a termite nest.
Then he called to the Karak-Karak women:
"My friends, come and see what I've found you!"

When they saw the termite nest
the excited spirit-women ran across
and began to tear it open with their bare hands.
But what a shock!
Before they could reach the termites,
the snakes came wriggling and hissing out at them!

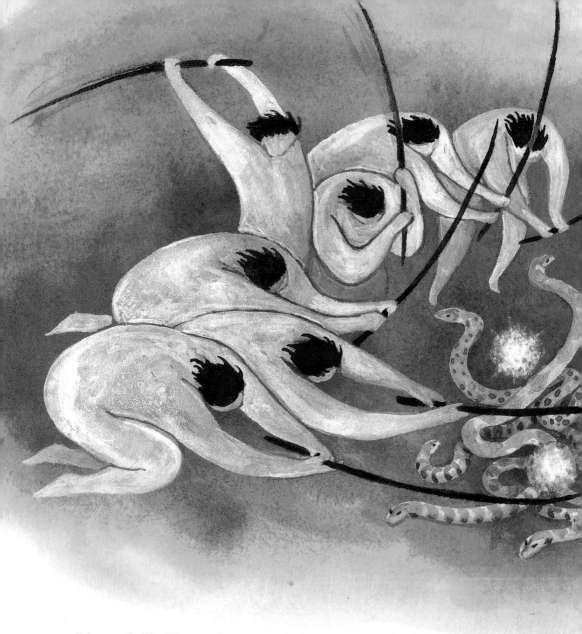

"Aaagh!" How those spirit-women screamed!
They attacked the snakes with their digging sticks:
Wham! Bam-bam!
They forgot all about the Fire hidden inside.
So each time they hit a snake,
a piece of sparkling flame
fell away from the ends of their sticks.

14

This was just what Wakala wanted.
He darted forward
and snatched up the flames for himself
between two pieces of bark.
"I've got it!" he shouted.
"Fire is mine now!"

When the last snake lay dead,
the Karak-Karak women stood there trembling.
Their digging-sticks had gone cold, so cold –
for all their Fire was gone.
They could see Wakala running off with it,
like a dark shadow carrying bright fragments of sun.

16

Slowly, slowly, the Karak-Karak women
turned cold too.
They did not want to stay on Earth
where bad men played such tricks on them.
So they lifted their hands
until the wind caught them
and carried them up to the sky.
There they turned into stars.

Meanwhile, back on Earth,
Wakala was really enjoying Fire.
He rubbed his hands in its warmth.
He threw great chunks of meat into it
until they were sizzling hot and delicious to eat.
He felt very pleased with himself!

18

But he was just as selfish
as the Karak-Karak women.
Every day, other people came and begged him,
"Hey, Wakala, please lend us some Fire."
"No," he yelled at them all,
"Wah, wah, wah! I won't, it's mine!"

Soon the other people grew so jealous and angry
that they started a big fight.
They attacked Wakala with stones and spears.
In return, he hurled burning coals at them ...
Oh, the fool!
The coals set fire to the grass -
a huge, spreading Fire!

With a great cheer,
everyone rushed forward
to catch some of this wonderful Fire for themselves.
Then they ran off with it in every direction,
carrying it back to their own camps.

Wakala couldn't believe what he had done.
He was so angry with himself
that he jumped into the roaring flames
and let them burn him right up!

But that wasn't the end of him.
For out of the ashes
he came to life again.
He was ash-black himself now,
a black crow,
still calling "Wah, wah, wah!"

Ever since then, yes, since the Dream-Time,
the Karak-Karak stars have shone in the night sky
and Wakala the crow has called his miserable
"Wah, wah, wah," through the day.
And ever since then
Fire has belonged to everyone.

24